Omnibus Press Presents

The Story of Alanis Morissette

Copyright © 1996 Omnibus Press
(A Division of Music Sales)

Written by Kalen Rogers
Designed by Amy MacIntyre

UK ISBN 0.7119.5984.6
US ISBN 0.8256.1548.8
UPC 7.52187.47847.8
Order No. OP 47847

Exclusive Distributors:

Music Sales Limited
8/9 Frith Street, London W1V 5TZ England

Music Sales Corporation
257 Park Avenue South, New York, NY 10010 USA

Music Sales Pty. Limited
120 Rothschild Street, Rosebery, Sydney,
NSW 2018, Australia

Photo Credits

Bill Becker/Canapress Photo Service
Page 13

Jay Blakesberg/Retna Ltd.
Pages 14 + 15, 24, 48

Kevin Cummins/London Features International
Front cover, page 1, 29

Bill Davila/Retna Ltd.
Pages 5, 38 + 39, 40

Gregg DeGuire/London Features International
Page 43

Steve Double/Retna Ltd.
Page 17

Nick Elgar/London Features International
Page 27

David Fisher/London Features International
Pages 44 + 45

Armando Gallo/Retna Ltd.
Pages 18 + 19, 24 + 25, 31

Niels Van Iperen/Retna Ltd.
Page 47

Dennis Kleiman/Retna Ltd.
Page 33

Gie Knaeps/London Features International
Page 46

Eddie Malluk/Retna Ltd.
Page 35

Jeffrey Mayer/Star File Photo
Pages 2 + 3, 21, 23

Kevin Mazur/London Features International
Pages 22, 26, 32, 41

Simon Meaker/Retna Ltd.
Page 16

Musto/London Features International
Page 11

Scarlet Page/Retna Ltd.
Back cover

Marco Shark/LGI Photo Agency
Pages 6, 12

Gene Shaw/Star File Photo
Pages 36 + 37

Kelly A. Swift/Retna Ltd.
Page 42

Davey Terrio/Retna Ltd.
Pages 10, 34

Printed in the United States of America by
Vicks Lithograph and Printing Corporation

INTRODUCTION

Alanis Morissette has proven that music that is at once exhilarating and unsettling does have a place in Top 10 land. Armed with a voice capable of sweet, breathless nothings and head-long howls of abandon, she is here to remind us of our innermost feelings. Her songs call up conflicting emotions—from spitting venom to introspective serenity—and bring them out into the light for all to see. Her multiplatinum album *Jagged Little Pill* is a therapist's dream, an ex-lover's nightmare, and a best friend for anyone who's ever felt confused and confounded.

Seeming to emerge from nowhere in 1995, the shadowy presence of the singer-songwriter with the inimitable voice and disconcerting lyrics became more and more recognizable as the year went on. In 1996 the twenty-one-year-old became a Grammy Award winner four times over. But Alanis did not gain her insight or develop her talent without her fair share of experience—including television acting at the age of ten and two Canadian album releases while she was still a teenager. It was when she found herself at rock bottom, her previous successes no more than a thorn in her side, that she began to take stock of it all and, with a clean slate, began the "spiritual experience" of writing the songs that would make up *Jagged Little Pill.*

An album full of stylistically diverse songs held together by a wonderfully unusual voice and brutally candid subject matter has been received with a sigh of relief by an audience weary of grunge and dissatisfied by the quick pick-me-up of punk and pop. The story of Alanis Morissette is as intruiging as her music; as she says, "*What it all comes down to/Is that I haven't got it all figured out just yet.*"

MEASURE UP

Alanis Nadine Morissette was born on June 1, 1974, in Ottawa, Canada, to a French-Canadian father, Alan, and a Hungarian-born mother, Georgia. The Morissettes' occupation of choice, military school teaching, moved Alanis, her twin brother Wade, and her older brother Chad around quite a bit; Alanis spent her early childhood in West Germany. Upon arriving back in Canada at age six, little Alanis decided to get into what would later become much more than a hobby and began playing the piano. A few years later she tired of singing other people's tunes and started to pen her own. By all accounts a precocious little number with goals far beyond those of her peers—a new Barbie doll just wasn't going to cut it for this one—Alanis landed herself a starring role on the Nickelodeon cable TV show *You Can't Do That on Television* at the ripe old age of ten. As she would years later tell *Rolling Stone* magazine, "It was a good, stupid, sarcastic kind of show. Very obnoxious and very tongue in cheek."

And very lucrative from a ten-year-old's perspective. But blow her hard-earned dough on video games and trips to the mall this preteen would not; she saved her paychecks until she had a tidy little sum and cut her own record. Two thousand copies of "Fate Stay with Me" were pressed on Lamor Records, Alanis's own independent label. "I want to prove to people

that just because you're young, it doesn't mean you can't do as much as adults can," she told *Ottawa* magazine in 1987. The now-familiar Morissette theme of jilted love is evident even this early in her songwriting career (*What did you think I'd be doing now/While you left me, I was thinking aloud/Would there be no end to my sorrow/Will I make it through tomorrow*). Either Alanis is a first-class prophesier or she had a nasty trip down lover's lane in a previous life.

It was around this time that Alanis hooked up with Stephan Klovan, a sort of organizer/producer of entertainment events in Ottawa. He came to the Morissette's house to "audition" twelve-year-old Alanis and her brother for the Springtime Tulip Festival. After Alanis refused to display her aptitude in the form of a requested cartwheel in the backyard and instead sang a little ditty she'd written entitled "Find the Right Man," Klovan cast her in the Festival and took her under his wing. He decided that the best way to jump-start the young singer's career would be by booking her gig after gig singing the Canadian national anthem at major sporting events—the *coup de grace* being the opening ceremonies of the 1988 World Figure Skating Championships. As he explained to the *Ottawa Sun* in 1996, he figured that singing in front of thousands of people "gave her a high level of confidence and exposure that is very beneficial for her now."

TEN THOUSAND SPOONS

Perhaps weary of belting out "O Canada" at the drop of a hat, Alanis began collaborating with musician Leslie Howe. He helped her to record a few tracks designed to put Alanis on TV again—this time on *Star Search*, a talent show on which she performed a cover version of the Osmonds song "One Bad Apple."

Spending most of her free time after classes at Glebe Collegiate high school in Howe's studio, Alanis was beginning to build up quite a repertoire of material. Klovan was busy getting his young talent gigs; he worked on her image by persuading local retailers to donate trendy clothes for the singer to wear while performing. Groomed and fine-tuned, Alanis was ready to shop her stuff to record labels. Klovan determined that presenting the usual demo tape just wasn't slick enough, and amazingly enough scraped together the funds to fly Alanis to Paris to film a video for her song "Walk Away." The combination of Morissette and the Eiffel Tower

proved to be irresistible to MCA A&R man John Alexander. As Howe put it, "He flipped out. And we signed."

In order to concentrate her overabundant energies on recording her first album, the fourteen-year-old decided to drop out of the New York Fries, the cover band she'd been singing with. The album was recorded at Distortion Studios in Ottawa during September through December 1990. In April of 1991, it was released with the simple title *Alanis*.

A baby-faced Alanis, decked out in black leather and with the requisite pout, graces the album cover. The sleeve notes include lengthy "thanks" from both Leslie Howe and Alanis to a variety of people. Alanis thanks her parents and brothers; to her twin brother Wade she says, "You've never doubted me and you've always stood by my side, even if that meant stepping out of the spotlight and letting *me* shine. If anyone deserves to shine it's *you*. I love you Wadee." The sleeve notes also include mutually appreciative notes between Howe and Alanis. Howe, then unaware of how successful his musical partner would become, writes, "Don't forget me when you're a big star and I'm just a loser producer having to make appointments just to talk to your manager's secretary's assistant in order to do your laundry." Alanis in turn thanks Howe for "giving me the chance to develop what I have—people like you are very rare."

Alanis with her parents

The ten tracks on the album are fairly straightforward dance/pop tunes, and the voice now known for its range from sweet whispers to howling rage is very rarely glimpsed. Song titles such as "Party Boy," "Superman," and "Jealous" all indicate that Alanis's present preoccupation with unsatisfying relationships is not a new one, but the lyrics themselves never rise above pop fluff and are no precursor to the blatant honesty showcased on *Jagged Little Pill*. Lines from "Oh Yeah!" (*My name is Alanis I'm just sixteen so/please gimme a break I'm no disco queen*), "Human Touch" (*with a toot in your snoot and your loot to boot/you don't even give a hoot about the minds you pollute*), and "Too Hot" (*Throw your hands in the air/And wave 'em like you just don't care*) are difficult to reconcile with the Grammy Award–winning Alanis of 1996, but, as she says, she was after all just sixteen. The first single, "Too Hot," was just that, and with the help of a little hairspray and a promotional tour, the future Angry Young Woman of Rock seemed set to be forever relegated to the land of Debbie Gibson. Breaking her busy promo schedule to open for Vanilla Ice in Ottawa and to pick up a Juno Award (Canada's answer to the Grammys) for "Most Promising Female Vocalist," Alanis found herself with a double platinum debut album.

Going back to high school after a summer filled with interviews, photo shoots, awards, and adulation was quite probably a more surreal experience for someone who'd been immersed in the entertainment industry since the age of ten than finding yourself Canada's own version of Tiffany. Suddenly surrounded by more friends than she knew what to do with, Alanis opted to hang out with the slightly more mature crowd she'd always seemed to gravitate toward, and even began dating a man allegedly twice her age in TV actor Dave Coulier of *Full House* and *America's Funniest People* fame.

Morissette's second album, *Now Is the Time*, came out in October 1992. The album's cover featured a much cooler looking Alanis than the previous year's release, but alas (or as luck would have it) the sophomore jinx apparently affects even the teen/dance/pop genre, and the album sold a barely respectable 50,000 copies.

Now Is the Time, both musically and lyrically, is a Janet Jackson *Rhythm Nation* type self-empowerment album. The sleeve notes begin with a photo of a pensive-looking Alanis beside an encouraging note from the artist to her fans ("Don't ever let anyone destroy who you are and what you believe") which closes with, "Never give up. Don't be afraid. I believe in you." The photographs that make up this album's artwork show a much more mature, womanly Alanis, albeit one who still had a penchant for big hair, big jewelry, and more than a fair share of eye makeup. The voice of *Jagged Little Pill* is still buried deep beneath the likes of the Celine Dionesque ballad "No Apologies" and the occasional Madonna soundalike in the bridges of "The Time of Your Life" and "Big Bad Love." The main theme remains men and love, although the sophomoric Alanis seems a bit more self-confident (*When you are beggin' me for money/Just got to tell me what you need/But if you want my lovin' buddy/You've got to get down on your knees*). The thank-yous for this album include a revealing note to "Jim (Puerta Allarta March '92 ... You never said good-bye)" along with a dedication to her family and a tribute to Leslie Howe, "the coolest dude in the universe."

INTELLECTUAL INTERCOURSE

In an effort to get the numbers up, in 1993 John Alexander contacted American-based Scott Welch of Atlas/Third Rail Management to propose U.S. releases of Morissette's two albums. Welch had to his credit catapulted the career of Paula Abdul, among others. He immediately squelched the idea of launching *Alanis* and *Now Is the Time* on an unsuspecting U.S. record-buying public, and advised Alanis to put her already wilting stint as a teen pop star under her bed along with her high school yearbook and get out of the house. She took his counsel and moved to Toronto to take in, as Welch put it, "new surroundings and new life experiences."

The surroundings turned out to be a small, cheap apartment and the experiences seemed centered around a seemingly endless revolving roster of prospective songwriting partners. After two years of fruitless collaboration with what Alanis now claims to have been "hundreds" of songwriters, she decided that an even more drastic uprooting was in the cards for her, and at the age of twenty picked up and moved to the City of Angels. Arriving in the sprawling metropolis of Los Angeles knowing only a handful of people, Alanis was initiated into life in la-la land via being robbed at gunpoint. As she would later tell *Spin* magazine in their November 1995 edition which featured her on the cover, "Leaving Toronto to go

to L.A. gave me a severe dose of disillusionment that was really necessary. I was finally in a position where things *weren't* working out. And it was good for me."

Los Angeles was the backdrop for a fated meeting between Alanis and songwriter/producer Glen Ballard. As arranged by their mutual publishing company MCA, Alanis arrived one day in February 1994 at Ballard's studio in Hollywood. Ballard, no novice to the music business, had worked with the likes of Quincy Jones; Barbra Streisand; Earth, Wind and Fire; and Aretha Franklin; he also cowrote the Michael Jackson hit "Man in the Mirror." As Ballard would later tell the *Ottawa Sun*, "She came to my studio, and we started writing about fifteen minutes later ... there was an instant rapport ... it was one of those instant connections." It seemed that Ballard was as ready for a new musical direction and a new creative outlook as Alanis was, and one simple meeting was the catalyst for a collaboration that would prove to be a successful and freeing experience for both of them. "There's no doubt it was a genuine and artistic awakening," Ballard recalls. He would later tell *Grammy Magazine*'s Spring 1996 edition, "I think God gave me Alanis so that I could explore a whole other side of me that was lying fallow." As Alanis told *Rolling Stone* magazine in their November 2, 1995 issue,

"It was the most spiritual experience either of us ever had with music. The whole thing was very accelerated and stream of consciousness."

The two songwriters then set out to write and record in what, indeed, seemed to be a stream of consciousness. Alanis has since stated that she would write and commit to tape a song and, upon arriving back at the studio the next day, have no recollection of it. The first song they penned together was called "The Bottom Line;" it and several others have never been released. Incredibly, all of the songs that would make up *Jagged Little Pill* were recorded in one or two takes right there in Ballard's studio. Alanis wrote all of the lyrics, and the two, both armed with acoustic guitars, created the music together which Ballard, an accomplished studio musician, committed to tape. Only a very few overdubs were added later—most notably the contribution of Red Hot Chili Peppers' Dave Navarro and Flea to "You Oughta Know." Little did Alanis and Ballard know that thirteen songs that were, essentially, demo tapes would become a Number 1 album.

Alternating time between her small apartment in Beachwood Canyon and Ballard's, Alanis opened her emotional floodgates and set to music exactly how she felt. Pent-up reactions to what life had so far offered her had before only surfaced in the form of anxiety attacks. As she would tell *Details* magazine in its October 1995, issue, when these attacks came on "I just bawled my eyes out and started shaking and wanted to faint. It scared the living shit out of me." She finally recognized that by facing up to her inner feelings, grabbing them by the throat, and dragging them out into the daylight, she could not only release the anger, betrayal, and confusion, but even come to appreciate it. As she reasoned to *Q* magazine, "I think you become a true adult when you can hit rock bottom and then walk away from that experience and transcend it." Recalling a breakthrough moment when she came to the realization that songwriting could be a way of purging and growing, she cites the first time she heard fellow artist Tori Amos's *Little Earthquakes* album, saying "I played the record in its entirety, lying on my living room floor, and I just bawled my eyes out ... I was so grateful."

Songwriter/producer
Glen Ballard at the
1996 Grammy Awards

RIGHT THROUGH YOU

Alanis, Ballard, and Scott Welch decided that the collection of songs was ready to leave the studio and venture out into the "real world" of major record labels. Alanis and her music were brought to the attention of Madonna's own Maverick Records by way of A&R man Guy Oseary. He reportedly agreed to set up a live performance screening of the unknown artist on the strength of a tape of the song "Perfect." Oseary, perhaps more open to the idea that talent and youthful determination can go hand-in-hand due to his own age of twenty-two, told *Spin* magazine that "people are always so amazed that we've accomplished anything, since Generation X-ers are supposedly not ambitious."

Regardless, it was Alanis's music that sealed a deal. Performing songs you've come to write after years of soul-searching and after having made it—and subsequently lost it—in the music business in front of record company bigwigs in their offices is not an easy task. But, as Scott Welch told the *Ottawa Sun*, "After half an hour they said 'That's enough. Let's go outside.' And we basically made the deal in the hallway."

Madonna, CEO of Maverick, has been widely quoted as saying that Alanis "reminds me of me when I started out: slightly awkward but extremely self-possessed and straightforward." Alanis has yet to draw such parallels, but told Chicago's WENZ during an August 1995, radio interview that the record label is "very focused on making the artist the priority" and applauded Maverick's hands-off approach as "they're very intent on signing people that have a really strong sense of their own identity."

In early 1995 the album entitled *Jagged Little Pill* was released. Featuring out-of-focus photographs and lyric pages that looked as if they'd come straight from a dusty old typewriter, its packaging didn't hint at the power inside. And so it was that a generation weaned on Nirvana's *Nevermind* and the ennui and discontent it represented, cheered up by the cartoonish do-it-yourself sound of Green Day, and used to the fact that female artists as diverse as Courtney Love and Björk do not have to be lumped together welcomed Alanis Morissette with open arms.

Here was a woman whose opening bid was a furious look-at-me-when-I'm-talking-to-you confrontation to a man who'd dumped her. Once the sound of Alanis's voice cut through Top 10 radio with questions like *"Are you thinking of me when you fuck her?"* and *"And every time I scratch my nails down someone else's back I hope you feel it... well can you feel it?"* jilted lovers the nation over sat up and listened. "You Oughta Know" became the summer's anthem, and as Alanis's

tortured vocals were played more and more over the airwaves, the growing curiosity about the girl behind the song sharpened.

Wisely, the video for "You Oughta Know" did nothing to dispel the mystery surrounding rock's new angry young woman. The shadowy, elusive figure of Alanis Morissette weaving through a desert may have been on MTV's high rotation, but it was not enough for music fans who, in an era when image is everything, were perhaps more accustomed to videos and photographs slapping them in the face rather than music and lyrics. Alanis' decision to rebel against an icon-hungry audience stemmed from her hard-earned outlook best expressed to *Grammy Magazine*; she says, "My whole philosophy on life is that I'm not about my external appearance. What I have to say is far more important than how long my eyelashes are."

Fans of "You Oughta Know" were delighted to discover that *Jagged Little Pill* exposed much more than just a pissed-off chick with one stock-in-trade emotion to voice. It seemed that it was not just her voice that was capable of covering the gamut of howling rage to sweet acceptance. The songs on the album leapt and dove through the mountainous region of human feelings and concerns. The hard-won

wisdom of "You Learn" (*I recommend getting your heart trampled on to anyone ... I recommend biting off more than you can chew to anyone*) goes hand-in-hand with the knowing sarcasm within "Not the Doctor" (*I don't want to be your glass of single malt whisky/Hidden in the bottom drawer*). There is room on the album for the hope and candor of "Head over Feet" (*You've already won me over in spite of me*). The often-whispered verses of "Perfect" recognize how damaging expectations of perfection can be (*Be a good girl/You've got to try a little harder/That simply wasn't good enough/to make us proud*). And in "Hand in My Pocket"—a song in which she claims to be both drunk and sober, brave and chicken shit—Alanis demonstrates that it is "fine fine fine" to have conflicting emotions, and that recognizing and appreciating them all—no matter how contradictory they may seem—may just balance you out. An uncredited *a cappella* song, a stark contrast to the driven mixture of harmonica, guitar, and drums that make up the first track, brings the album to a close with the sweet confessional plea of "*Would you forgive me love?*"

THROW IT DOWN

A tour, booked before management had any idea how hugely popular their newest artist would become, was underway and the ever-exploding number of fans bought tickets as soon as they went on sale. Alanis and her band were playing tiny venues to sold out crowds who'd already memorized every word on her barely released album. The star of the show was still so unrecognizable that ticketless fans were approaching her outside her own gigs to ask not for autographs but for any spare tickets she might have for sale.

The band—none of whom had had a hand in the creation of the music in Ballard's studio—were, Alanis contends, meant to be together. It does somehow seem suitable that she should be backed by four hairy rockers who can play the hell out of anything. Formerly of the band Mother Tongue,

guitarist Jesse Tobias was referred to Alanis by the Red Hot Chili Peppers' Dave Navarro who replaced Tobias after his own brief stint with the Peppers. Together with guitarist Nick Lashley, bassist Chris Chaney, and drummer Taylor Hawkins, they form a band that seems to fit as well musically as they do personally with their frontwoman. As Alanis told *Spin*, "If I wasn't in a band with them I probably would've dated each one of them already."

Keeping her head about her as her album continued to sell and sell, Alanis and company travelled from gig to gig in a small tour bus. Dressed in black leather, oversized men's shirts, miscellaneous flowing bits and pieces and with her long, dark hair whipping around her makeup-free face, Alanis cut a striking figure on stage by her sheer refusal to try. Her live persona was

labeled "asexual" but "mesmerizing" by critics. As Q magazine put it, "Truly, she oozes all the disregard for pop etiquette of a nonchalant veteran." Which makes all the sense in the world for someone who spent their formative years being groomed as a disco diva whose sole goal it was to entertain. By remaining grounded and playing small shows night after night, Alanis was proving that her music was the real thing. When Sinéad O'Conner had to drop out of the Summer of 1995 Lollapalooza tour due to her pregnancy, Alanis deftly turned down the much sought-after replacement slot. Not unaware of the pitfall of getting too big too fast, she decided to stick to Plan A. And much to her delight, it seemed to be working.

It was in the video for the second single "Hand in My Pocket" that Alanis seemed to decide to let the world see her face. Filmed on a Brooklyn, New York City, street block, the black-and-white video shows Alanis driving a Cadillac through a parade. The lazy, contented feeling the song evokes is captured very well in the slightly surreal visual. The video is directed by Mark Kohr, perhaps best known for the manic videos he put together for Green Day. The guys in the Morissette band make anonymous appearances as parade bystanders. Alanis herself projects a simple, "here I am—no pretenses" type of image.

The "Ironic" video, however, seems to be Alanis's final acquiescence to her fan's curiosity. Her formerly shadowy, hidden self which came physically to light in the "Hand in My Pocket" video was now completely out in the open for all to see. The video showcases Alanis's four alter-egos, all riding together in a beat-up old car. The

girl at the driver's seat is in control, keeping the car on the road and checking on the naughtier Alanises in the back seat via the rearview mirror. The four girls wear different color sweaters and slightly different hair (one has pigtails, one a woolen hat), but it is through their varied expressions as they all sing along to "*Who would've thought ... it figures*" that it is apparent that they each represent various facets of her personality. From the demure, introspective girl who throws an occasional tantrum to the teasing quirky child to the irresponsible passenger hanging out the window, all of these versions of Alanis Morissette are enjoying the trip and looking forward to where they're going. Even if the car does run out of gas.

UNCONDITIONAL THINGS

It was at the 1995 Grammy Awards that the music industry officially recognized what eight million American record-buyers already knew. Nominated for six Grammys—Album of the Year, Song of the Year, Best New Artist, Best Female Rock Performance, Best Rock Song, and Best Rock Album—Alanis walked up to the podium four times to accept awards. Winning over the likes of industry sweetheart Mariah Carey, Michael Jackson, Pearl Jam, and Hootie and the Blowfish—a band that has sold more albums than God—is not to be taken lightly.

Perhaps more impressive even than her four awards, however, was Alanis's stunning performance at the ceremonies. Seated on a high stool on a stage dimly lit by candlelabras and strewn with dark-red long-stemmed roses, her long black skirt echoing her snakelike hair, she sang "You Oughta Know" backed by acoustic guitars and a string section. The fury and abandon she usually displayed when performing the song was contained, quieted, but this made the lines *"Does she know how you told me you'd hold me/Until you died, 'til you died/But you're still alive"* even more bone-chilling.

Jagged Little Pill jumped back into Billboard's Number 1 slot after the award show was aired on February 28, 1996, and the album topped the charts in the U.K. and Australia. Alanis Morissette was not without her detractors,

however; not everybody likes a winner. Canadian journalists slagged their fellow-countrywoman off for having grown and developed since her pop diva days, labeling her a fake and a record label invention. *Swing* magazine featured a photo of Alanis on its May, 1996, cover with the header "Who's Killing Alternative Music?" and called her "alternative credentials"—initially intact due to her "willingness to sing about fellatio"—into question and claimed that many believe that she has "perverted the meaning of the term" by selling millions of records. The Internet has a site solely committed to disliking the singer/song-writer called People Against Alanis Morissette's Music (P.A.A.M.M. to insiders).

Alanis's decision not to allow MCA to reissue her first two albums—now only available in a few Canadian collectors' shops filed under "rare" and priced accordingly—was greeted with mixed response. Some applauded her for refusing to cash in on fans who would surely be disappointed if they were expecting two more *Jagged Little Pill*s. Others asserted that this served only to verify their contention that she was a fraud. As Alanis herself reasoned to *Q* magazine, "I think it was misconstrued as my being ashamed of it... How can I possibly spend the next eighty years of my life feeling bad about who I was or what I was doing when I was sixteen years old?"

So Alanis carries on playing for packed-out crowds around the world. And enjoying it. Being herself is the goal, and this includes her own brand of "sex, drugs, and rock 'n roll" behavior. She doesn't drink, smoke, do drugs, or start the day off with a cup of coffee. She doesn't read magazines, watch TV, or surf the net either. She does go into her own frenzied world on stage, howl like a lunatic, run like mad toward her audiences, and frighten even the bravest mosher. She also admits to being a very sexual being. For a twenty-one year old artist whose true debut album has sold over eight million copies, she has remained genuine and honest. But don't be lulled into a false sense of security. Now that you've swallowed all that *Jagged Little Pill* has to offer and are just beginning to digest it, be forewarned: Alanis has started writing again. One thing is certain—her next collection of songs will be creative, passionate, and most definitely something unexpected.

ALBUM DISCOGRAPHY

ALANIS
Feel Your Love / Too Hot / Plastic /
Walk Away / On My Own /
Superman / Jealous / Human Touch /
Oh Yeah! / Party Boy
MCA Records MCAD-10253

NOW IS THE TIME
Real World / An Emotion Away /
Rain / The Time of Your Life /
No Apologies / Can't Deny / When
We Meet Again / Give What You
Got / (Change Is) Never a Waste
of Time / Big Bad Love
MCA Records MCAD-10731

JAGGED LITTLE PILL
All I Really Want / You Oughta
Know / Perfect / Hand In My Pocket
/ Right Through You / Forgiven /
You Learn / Head Over Feet /
Mary Jane / Ironic /
Not the Doctor / Wake Up
Maverick Records 9 45901-2